CABIN FEVER RELIEVERS

Hundreds of Games, Activities, and Crafts for Creative Indoor Fun

By Tina Koch and
Mary-Lane Kamberg

Redleaf Press
A division of Resources for Child Caring

No part of this book is intended to conflict with existing child care laws or licensing regulations. Readers are responsible for compliance with laws and regulations governing child care and family child care licensing, as well as for ensuring the safety of the children in their care.

Cover illustration by Taia Morley, Minneapolis, Minnesota
Interior illustrations by Christine Tripp, Ontario, Canada

Published by: Redleaf Press
                  A division of Resources for Child Caring
                  450 North Syndicate, Suite 5
                  St. Paul, Minnesota 55104

Library of Congress Cataloging-in-Publication Data

Koch, Tina, 1943-
     Cabin fever relievers : hundreds of games, activities, and crafts
you can use for creative indoor fun / by Tina Koch and Mary-Lane
Kamberg.
          p. cm.
     ISBN 1-884834-28-0   (alk. paper)
     1. Indoor games. 2. Handicraft. 3. Creative activities and seat
work. I. Kamberg, Mary-Lane, 1948- II. Title.
GV1229.K63   1997
793--dc21   97-5618
                                                      CIP

Dedication

To my granddarlings, Christopher, Eric, Alex, Elizabeth, Allison, Andrew, Abigail, and Samuel, who inspire me to think like a child so I can continue to create for children everywhere.

—Tina Koch

To my husband Ken, who supports and encourages my life's work.

—Mary-Lane Kamberg

Acknowledgments

The authors would like to thank the following people for contributing their ideas, talents, encouragement, and support to the creation and preparation of this book:

The staff at The Day Care Connection: Valerie Cable, Kevin Cable, Sharon Yohn, Dana Worley, Alison Smith, Kay Rhodelander, Marti Lee, Vi Freeborn, Marcie Fallik, Cheryl Carter, Lou Capps, Billie Bopp, and Valerie Bielsker. Thanks also to Dick Hosty, Cathy Hair, Judy Clouston, Fred Ladewig, Jessie Ladewig, Becky Kamberg, Johanna Kamberg, Leslie Eden, The Whole Person, The Kansas City Writers Group, Mary Steiner Whelan, Mary Pat Merabella, Ronna Hammer, Paul Woods, Christina Tripp, Taia Morley, and Jan Grover.

Table of Contents

A Letter from Tina Koch

Is it raining? Snowing? Scorching hot? Arctic cold? And does that mean you and your family child care children must stay inside today? If so, perhaps you're wondering what you can do on a bad weather day.

I'd love to share some ideas with you. Over the years I spent as a family child care provider, I used simple ideas for creative indoor fun. Often all I needed to play games, create crafts, and entertain the children in my care were materials I already had on hand.

If I were there with you, we could create a yummy snack, or make a "Marvelous Mosaic." Or how about a game of "The Queen Has Lost Her Sparkles" or "Indoor Tetherball"?

I wish I could be there to jump, cut, paste, cook, and create fun with all of you. This book is the next best thing. I hope these ideas for every room in your home help you enjoy bad weather days with the children in your care. I will be there in spirit, riding on the children's laughter. Thank you for welcoming me into your home.

Tina Koch

October

In October's freezing days
I will not go out and play
For it is way too cold to play
Outside

—Johanna Kamberg
Age 10

Indoors

Outdoors is where I love to lurk
But at times it just won't work
Sometimes it rains and gets so wet
Can we be happy inside? You bet!

—Eric Hansen
Age 10

Floor Plan:
How to Use This Book

Wherever you live, a bad weather day sometimes keeps you indoors with the children in your care. You can't change what's going on outside. But you can create a change of scenery inside with plenty of ideas for something new to do.

Cabin Fever Relievers is designed as an easy-to-use resource for busy caregivers like you. Read it in one sitting, if you have time. Or flip it open at random for a quick idea when rain or snow unexpectedly interrupts your outdoor fun.

Here are hundreds of simple ideas you can use to enjoy time spent indoors. The book takes you from room to room as you lead children in a variety of games, crafts, and other activities.

Each chapter contains ideas for a specific room in your home. Chapter 1 (Kitchen) has ideas for quick, creative snacks that children can help you make. Many of these ideas include components of the U.S. Department of Agriculture's Child and Adult Care Food Program (CACFP). Where possible, these are indicated for you. Chapter 2 continues with kitchen ideas that include "Make a Mess" crafts that are too messy for other rooms. Spread out lots of newspapers and use the kitchen sink to keep cleanup time to a minimum.

Chapter 3 (Dining Room) includes ideas for games and crafts that need a table surface. And ideas in chapter 4 (Living Room) let children express their creativity through creative dramatics, storytelling, movement, and music.

You'll help children use their imaginations with activities for the bedroom and bathroom in chapter 5 (Bed and Bath). These ideas add excitement by using rooms children usually don't use for play.

Children need a physical way to use their boundless energy, especially on a bad weather day. Chapter 6 (Garage) has ideas for active movement that lets children bounce, jump, and run without venturing outside.

The last chapter is "The Room in Your Heart." It contains ideas for crafts children can make to give as gifts. It also includes activities that help children learn to care and share and to be sensitive to people with disabilities.

The end of each chapter features a section called "Your Own Ideas." Use this space to add crafts, games, or activities you create yourself, pick up at training workshops, or hear about from other caregivers or other sources.

Watch for this symbol!

IMPORTANT SAFETY TIP

Whenever a craft or activity is followed by this warning, be sure to read and follow the safety tip. These are critically important tips that help you ensure the health and safety of the children in your care.

1

Kitchen, Part I:
Junior Chefs

Creative cookery means indoor fun when weather dampens your enthusiasm for outdoor activities. Children can help you make culinary delights: unusual meals and snacks that are sure to be new favorites. Save these for "special days," when blowing snow or pouring rain gives you a little extra time to enjoy food preparation.

Monster Pancakes

Make a batch of pancake batter according to your own recipe or the directions on a packaged mix. Divide the batter into four bowls. Let the children help you add a different color of food coloring to each bowl, and stir. Preheat griddle or skillet. Let the children watch you drizzle a spoonful of each color onto the griddle so that all the colors touch. You'll have one monster pancake. Make one for each child. Leftover pancakes can be wrapped, refrigerated, and reheated another day.

IMPORTANT SAFETY TIP:

Be sure to protect children from hot griddle and cooking utensils to avoid burns.

Rainbow Cake

Chase away rainy-day blues with a rainbow cake the children help you make. Use a white cake mix, plastic resealable bags, and food coloring. After you mix the cake as directed on the package, divide the prepared batter into plastic resealable bags—one for each child. Add two drops of food coloring to each bag and close securely. Let the children squeeze the color into the batter. One at a time, snip a corner of each bag and let the child squeeze the batter into the prepared cake pan. Bake as directed. Although cake is not reimbursable on CACFP, you can use it for an occasional treat.

Cone-a-Copia

Let the children help you create a unique "summer" snack any day of the year. Use 16 ounces of flavored yogurt, 1 can of fruit cocktail, 6 marshmallows, and 6 flat-bottomed ice-cream cones. (Serves six.) Drain fruit cocktail in a colander, then lay it on several thicknesses of paper towel to soak up the rest of the juice. Gently fold the fruit into the yogurt. Have the children place a large marshmallow (not a miniature one) in the bottom of the cone to keep it from getting soggy. Then let them spoon the yogurt mixture into the cone, and eat. Yogurt and fruit cocktail are reimbursable on CACFP.

Pudding in a Pouch

Here's a fun, but messy, pudding-and-graham-cracker snack that children love. Use a small box of sugarless instant pudding for every four children. You'll also need milk, a resealable plastic bag for each child, and a box of graham crackers. Give each child a bag containing a generous tablespoon of pudding mix and $1/2$ cup milk. Be sure to squeeze the air out of the bag and zip it closed. Show the children how to hold the top and bottom of the bag and to shake vigorously for 2 minutes. Set the bags upright in the refrigerator for at least 30 minutes. (The mix will look thin at first, but it will thicken.) When ready, give each child several graham crackers on a plate. Snip $1/4$ inch from the corner of each bag and let the children squeeze the pudding onto the crackers. Add a glass of juice for each child, and you have a healthy snack. Graham crackers and juice are reimbursable on CACFP.

Topsy-Turvy Lunch

Make an ordinary lunch exciting with unusual serving ideas:

- Color mashed potatoes pink.
- Serve milk in coffee cups.
- Put spaghetti sauce on the plate first and top with pasta.
- Use a straw to drink tomato soup.
- Cut carrots in circles instead of sticks.
- Pair up the children and let them feed each other.
- Create your own wacky ideas for a lunch the children will remember.

Stone Soup

Teach the children about sharing by combining story time with lunch preparation (and a little advance planning). First, get a copy of the story *Stone Soup* by Ann McGovern (New York: Scholastic, 1986) at your library or bookstore. Ask each child's parent to contribute an assigned fresh vegetable on "Stone Soup Day." Also ask each parent to send an empty plastic container with a lid. In the morning, read the story together. Tell the children you are going to prepare stone soup using the vegetables they brought. Put several whole scrubbed potatoes in a big pot and tell the children they are the pretend stones. Then, following the pattern in the story, prompt the children to offer their vegetable contributions. Let the children help you wash the fresh vegetables and cut them up, using safe knives. Add a few beef bouillon cubes, $1\frac{1}{2}$-pounds precooked ground beef, a 46-ounce can of vegetable juice, and several cups of water. Cook on medium heat until vegetables are tender. Serve the stone soup for lunch with corn bread or biscuits. Ladle the remainder into the parents' containers to take home. Stone soup furnishes the protein and two vegetable components of CACFP.

IMPORTANT SAFETY TIP:
Never leave children alone with knives or other kitchen utensils.

Tutti-Frutti Pops

Cut bananas into 1-inch chunks and have the children place one chunk in the bottom of a 3- to 5-ounce paper cup. Push a popsicle stick into the banana so the stick stands up. Pour in orange or pineapple juice. Freeze and enjoy. The banana and juice count as one fruit on CACFP.

Apple De-"Lights"

Use flavored apple rings to teach the children about traffic safety while they enjoy a quick snack. You'll need apples, 3 cups of cold water, 3 saucepans, and 3 packages of flavored gelatin (one each of red, green, and yellow). Peel, core, and cut enough thick apple slices so that each child gets three apple rings. In separate pans, mix each package of gelatin with 1 cup water. When the gelatin granules dissolve, lay an equal number of apple rings flat in each pan. Simmer on top of the stove until gelatin thickens. Let apples cool in the pan, then put one of each color on each child's plate in the same order as a traffic light: red, yellow, and green. Talk about crossing streets safely as everyone enjoys the treat. Add a glass of milk for a healthy snack. The apple is the fruit component on CACFP, and the milk is the liquid component.

Picasso Pizza

Give each child a flattened, unbaked biscuit (either homemade or from a commercially prepared refrigerated tube). Place them on small squares of aluminum foil. With a permanent marker, write each child's name on the edge of the foil. Let each child spread 1 tablespoon of pizza sauce on top of the biscuit, then sprinkle with 1 rounded tablespoon of shredded mozzarella or other cheese. Give the children a selection of sliced and diced pizza ingredients, such as hot dogs, precooked ground beef, mushrooms, onions, black olives, or even chunks of pineapple. Let them create their own works of art. Older children may want to use the ingredients to make funny faces. Bake on a cookie sheet at 350° F for about 12 minutes, or according to biscuit recipe or package directions. This counts as bread and protein on CACFP.

IMPORTANT SAFETY TIP:
Hot dogs and vegetables can be a choking hazard. Be sure pieces are small enough so they do not get caught in a child's throat.

4

Inside-Out Sandwich

Give each child a crunchy (baked) bread stick. Children spread cheese on the bread stick from a jar of spreadable cheese or a can of "squeeze" cheese. Then they wrap a 1-ounce slice of lunch meat around the bread stick, and eat. (The cheese is sticky and holds the meat in place.) Bread and meat count on CACFP.

Have a Bug for Lunch

Bugs are fun to eat, especially when they're really raisins. Let the children spread peanut butter on two cheese crackers. Then place a raisin "bug" on one side and tell them to press the crackers together for a "bug" sandwich. Milk is nice with this snack. Serve enough "bug" sandwiches to count as a bread and peanut butter sandwich on CACFP.

Arts and Crafts Snacks

Use a whole graham cracker or cooked, toaster-sized waffle as the canvas for a work of food art that children create and eat. Children spread peanut butter or flavored cream cheese on the cracker or waffle. Give them an assortment of decorative tidbits like raisins, pretzels, puffed oat cereal, or other foods. Have them create ready-to-eat funny faces or free-form designs. Add a glass of milk or fruit juice for a healthy snack.

The Crunch Bunch

Tempt children with this crunchy, nutritious apple snack. Cut apples in half and remove the cores with a melon baller. Give the children a dollop of peanut butter, puffed rice cereal, and grated carrots. Let them mix all ingredients and spread on the apple halves. Or spread peanut butter on the apple first and let the children sprinkle on the rest of the ingredients one at a time.

Funny Bunny

Use drained, canned pear halves and peach slices to make a funny bunny that children love to eat as a snack, salad, or dessert. Give each child a pear half and two peach slices. Let them position the fruit on a lettuce leaf, using the pear for the bunny's face and the peach slices for ears. Use raisins for eyes, a cherry or half a red grape for the nose, and six pretzel sticks stuck into the pear for whiskers (three on each side of the face). Talk about foods that rabbits eat, including the lettuce that the children's bunnies are resting on.

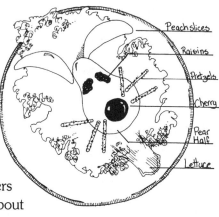

Banana Bites

Cut a banana in half the long way and place the flat edge on a paper plate. Smear peanut butter on the curved edge and cut into bite-sized pieces. Let the children sprinkle raisins, coconut, or pieces of their favorite cold cereal onto the banana bites. Serve with milk.

Eggs-Citing Eggs

Use tempera paints to decorate hard-boiled eggs to eat for lunch or to take home. Hard-boil an egg for each child. Then seat the children around the table and put a cake pan or pie plate in front of each one. Put a cooled egg in each pan. Using the tip of a spoon, dribble a small amount of paint into each pan and have the children gently roll the eggs around the pan to pick up color. Repeat several times with different colors. Let dry. Serve with juice.

Eggs-Citing Eggs, II

Hard-boil an egg for each child. Using cellophane tape or small adhesive stickers of various shapes (star stickers work very well), have the children place shapes in a random pattern on the eggs. Then use food coloring to dye the children's eggs their favorite colors. (To make egg dye from food coloring, add $1/4$ teaspoon food coloring and 2 teaspoons distilled vinegar to $2/3$ cup boiling water. Cool. Use a slotted spoon to dip eggs.) When eggs are dry, the children can peel off the stickers to reveal the designs made by the white shell underneath.

❗ IMPORTANT SAFETY TIP:
To avoid burns, be sure the dye is cool before letting children dip their eggs.

Circus Wheels

For a fruit snack that's bursting with flavor, peel and slice bananas into $1/2$-inch-thick circles. Using toothpicks, the children can spear the banana slices, dip them in milk, and place them flat on plates. Then they can sprinkle different colors of flavored gelatin crystals onto them. Add a glass of milk for a healthy snack.

Homemade Peanut Butter

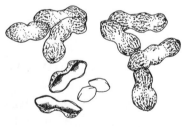

Divide a pound of unshelled roasted peanuts among the children. Let them crack the shells, remove the skins, and put the nuts in the blender a handful at a time. Blend on low, then puree until peanut butter reaches desired consistency. Dribble vegetable oil or peanut oil in the blender to moisten. Add salt to taste. Return blender setting to low as the children add each handful of peanuts. Serve the peanut butter right away. Refrigerate any leftovers.

❗ IMPORTANT SAFETY TIP:
Peanuts can be a choking hazard. Watch younger children carefully.

Fruit Kabobs

Get ready for lunchtime fun with fruit kabobs that the children make themselves. Give the children party stir sticks and let them spear grapes, maraschino cherries, and chunks of apple, banana, and pineapple. For extra fun, add small cubes of cheese or ham.

❗ IMPORTANT SAFETY TIP:
Food in chunks can be a choking hazard for young children. Don't serve to children younger than age three.

Fun Dip

Serve plain yogurt in individual cups and sprinkle flavored gelatin crystals or pudding powder on top. Children stir the mixture, then use graham cracker quarters to dip out the yummy snack.

Rainbow Snack

Give the children graham cracker squares spread with softened cream cheese. Give them three or four colors of flavored gelatin crystals to sprinkle in arc shapes, making multicolored rainbows on the cream cheese. A cup of orange or apple juice adds a pot of gold at the end of the rainbow for a healthy snack.

Fruit Pops

Let the children help you make a frozen treat they'll love to eat. Spoon canned fruit cocktail (with syrup or natural juice) into 5-ounce paper cups, two-thirds full. Wedge popsicle sticks between pieces of fruit so they stand up. Freeze. Remove fruit pops from paper cups and serve with milk or graham crackers for a healthy snack.

Nibble Necklace

Give each child a new shoelace long enough to form a circle that fits over the child's head. Tie a big knot at one end of the shoelace. Set out a bowl of Cheerios cereal and one of Fruit Loops cereal. Children string pieces of cereal to within 3 inches of the end. Tie a loop in the end of the shoelace and hook it over the knot to fasten the necklace. Add a glass of milk for a fun, healthy snack that children can eat right off the necklaces they're wearing. Add more cereal for a complete snack.

"Grate" Snacks!

Children have fun helping make these delicious snacks. Preheat oven to 350° F. Place a square of aluminum foil for each child on a cookie sheet. Be sure the children's hands are clean. Then give them a dab of shortening to spread on the foil, or spray each square with a vegetable oil spray. Place refrigerated biscuits on the foil squares and have the children press them into flat circles. Grate enough apples and cheese for everyone and mix with raisins in a bowl. Pass the bowl and let the children spoon the mixture onto the biscuits and spread it to cover the whole biscuit. Bake 10 to 12 minutes. Cool for a few minutes and serve warm with glasses of cold milk.

Mishmash

Children use mashed potatoes to create edible art. Make one serving of instant mashed potatoes for each child. Divide potatoes into three or four bowls. Add four to six drops of food coloring to each bowl. Place colored potatoes in resealable plastic bags. Cut off a bottom corner of each bag and let children take turns squeezing potatoes onto paper plates to make pictures or designs. When completed, they're ready to eat. Potatoes are a CACFP lunch vegetable component. At snack time, add a glass of milk.

Your Own Ideas

Use this space to write your own fun ideas.

Chapter

2

Kitchen, Part II:
The Mess in Your Mess Hall

G o ahead. Make a mess! Isn't that what mess halls are for? Maybe not every day, but on a dreary, stay-inside day, it's time for a change of pace. Spread out newspapers and assemble whatever you'll need for easy cleanup. Then let the games and crafts begin!

Name Fame

Create each child's name in sparkling lights using poster board, flat tooth-picks, glue, and several colors of glitter. Arrange the flat toothpicks to form each child's name in block letters. Position the name on a piece of poster board, leaving at least a 1-inch border on all four sides. Help chil-dren glue toothpicks to the poster board. Let dry. Let the children use another toothpick to dab glue onto one letter and then sprinkle glitter over it. (Do this over paper plates so you can easily save the excess glitter.) Use other glitter colors on the other letters. Let dry and send home for children to put on the doors to their rooms.

Sweet-Smelling Names

Explore the sense of smell by creating a work of "aroma art." Print each child's name on butcher paper. Use a couple of drops of water to thin a saucerful of white glue. Let the children dip paint brushes in the glue and trace over their names. Then have them sprinkle different flavors of granular gelatin (not sugar-free) on each letter. Set aside to dry. Each letter will have its own distinctive aroma.

Pasta Palaces

Create a cottage collage using a variety of uncooked pasta shapes, construction paper, and glue. Put bowls filled with different kinds of pasta in the center of a table but within the children's reach. Let the children design a house by arranging pieces of pasta on a sheet of construction paper. They can use spaghetti sticks to form the framework, elbow macaroni for curved places, and spiral pasta for bushes or chimney smoke. Older children may want to add trees or people in the yard. Encourage the children's creativity. When the houses are ready, let the children glue the pasta in place. Save any leftover pasta for future projects.

❗ IMPORTANT SAFETY TIP:
Items used in this craft are too small for children under age three.

Macaroni Match

Turn a simple matching game into a work of art. First collect a variety of uncooked pasta, bits of large-sized cereal, and dried beans. Give each child a cereal bowl of these assorted food shapes. Use a muffin tin or several paper muffin cups to help the children sort their pieces. In each empty muffin cup, place one example of each item. Have the children select items from their cereal bowls and say, "Eenie, Meenie, Minie, Moe. Where, oh, where, does this one go?" Each child then places her item in the proper muffin cup. When the game is over, the children can make a collage out of the food shapes, arranging the items on pieces of construction paper and gluing them in place. Save any unused materials for future projects.

❗ IMPORTANT SAFETY TIP:
Items used in this craft are too small for children under age three.

Corny Craft

Make a corny food collage using popped and
unpopped kernels of corn. You'll need popcorn, construction paper, a marker, scissors,
and glue. Use a marker to draw a corn cob
shape about 5 inches long in the middle of a
piece of construction paper. Give the children
corn kernels to glue onto the shape. Cut strips
of green construction paper about 4 inches
long. Have children glue on two strips so they
look like the corn's husk. Then draw several
curved lines away from the ear and let children
glue popped corn at the end of the curves.
Save the unused corn for future projects.

IMPORTANT SAFETY TIP:

Items used in this craft are too small for children under age three.

What's This For?

Kitchen utensils are game pieces for this easy activity. Place a wide variety
of kitchen tools in the center of the table: rolling pin, sifter, spatula, hot
mitt, saucepan, muffin tin, ladle, cookie sheet, etc. Have the children sit
around the table. First ask them to name all the items as you point to
them. Then ask questions like "What's this for?" and "I'm going to make
muffins. What do I need?" Continue asking until all the items have been
pointed to. Now let the children make up the questions. For interesting
variations, let the children use their creativity by asking, "How can you use
this in a way other than what it's usually used for?" Encourage unconven-
tional uses.

Create a Meal

Give each child a paper plate. Using different colors of construction paper, a marker, and scissors, cut simple shapes to resemble chicken legs, fish sticks, veggie burgers, bread, apples, bananas, oranges, grapes, carrots, green beans, peas, milk, cheese, etc. Let the children choose their favorite foods and glue them to their plates. Using food pyramid guidelines, help the children create a balanced meal. To order a copy of the booklet *The Food Label, the Pyramid, and You,* send a check or money order for $1.25 to the Superintendent of Documents, Consumer Information Center, Department 119-C, Pueblo, Colorado 81009. Or ask your CACFP sponsor for a free copy of the food pyramid booklet. The reference desk of your library can also help you find a copy.

Spring Fever

What's better than a breath of spring on a wintry day? Why not create blossoming fruit trees. You'll need a book with color pictures of fruit trees in bloom. Other supplies include scissors, glue, construction paper (blue, brown, and green), and tissue paper (white, pink, or yellow). Use the pictures in the book as you talk about how fruit trees blossom before fruit develops. Then let the children "grow" their own trees. Have the children cut 1-inch-wide strips of brown paper into varying lengths to use for tree trunks and branches. Then let the children cut leaf shapes from green construction paper. They can glue the tree trunks and branches onto the blue paper, then add the leaves. Cut 1-inch squares of tissue paper for blossoms. Let the children crumple the tissue squares and glue them onto the branches. The tissue squares will slightly uncrumple to look very much like a fruit tree in spring. Help children draw a bee or two for extra fun. If you care for school-age children, let them use real sticks and branches from your yard. Put a collection of branches in a vase for display.

❗ IMPORTANT SAFETY TIP:
Be sure to use child-safe scissors and supervise their use.

Pussy Willow Pictures

Instead of trees, you and the children can make pussy willows. Follow directions in the previous activity, but cut ½-inch-wide brown stems instead of tree trunks. Omit the leaves and substitute puffed rice cereal for the tissue paper. If you like, have the children draw a vase or cut one out of green construction paper. You'll be amazed at the lifelike results.

Caterpillar Colors

Cut 2-inch-wide strips from the short side of a sheet of construction paper. Show the children how to make a paper chain by linking the strips together with glue. The children may choose a different color for each link. On the last link, they can draw two eyes and glue on two thin black strips of paper for the caterpillar's antennae. Use the completed caterpillar to teach the children colors. For example, focus on one color each day, describing other items in the room that have the same color. When everyone is ready, move on to the next color. As soon as all the children know their colors, they may take their caterpillars home.

Fantastic Flurries

Create an indoor snowstorm of sparkling snowflakes using flat toothpicks, blue construction paper, glue, and silver or white glitter. Talk about the way snowflakes sparkle as the children position toothpicks onto the paper in a snowflake design. (You may want to cut some of the toothpicks in half for more variety.) When the designs are completed, the children glue the toothpicks into place. Then they dip a toothpick into the glue and carefully cover each toothpick of the snowflake. Children then sprinkle with glitter. When dry, shake off the excess to reveal a lovely snowflake.

Butterflies Are Free

Don't wait for spring to let butterflies brighten the day. The children can make their own with white typing paper, tempera paint, paintbrushes, and scissors. Help the children fold a sheet of paper in half, then help them drip drops of paint onto only the left half of the paper (inside the fold). While the paint is still wet, have the children fold the dry half over the wet side and gently rub the back of the dry side to spread the paint inside the paper. Wait a minute and have the children open the paper to dry. When the paper is dry, they can fold the paper again and draw one-half of a butterfly on one-half of the backside of the paper so that the fold becomes the butterfly's body. Children can cut along the line and open their papers to reveal beautiful butterflies. You may want to read them the story *The Very Hungry Caterpillar* by Eric Carle (New York: Philomel Books, 1994).

Spuds in Duds

Have the children make their own Potato Head family with one medium-sized, washed potato for each child. Give each child a 2-by-8-inch strip of cardboard, toothpicks, buttons, pipe cleaners, markers, and glue. Print each child's name on the cardboard strip and bend the strip into a circle. Staple in place to form a collar. Older children can print their own names and do their own stapling. Let the children decorate the potatoes to look like people by gluing on their choice of craft supplies. When dry, set the potatoes upright in the collars.

❗ IMPORTANT SAFETY TIP:
Items used in this craft are too small for children under age three.

A Place of My Own

Children will enjoy making and using these pretty place mats that show them where to put their plates, spoons, forks, napkins, and drinking cups or glasses. You will need construction paper, clear contact paper (or access to a laminator), scissors, glue, and shapes to trace: circles for plates and cups, rectangles or triangles for napkin, a spoon, and a fork. You will also need a roll of wallpaper or large sheets of construction paper for the place mat background. Let the children select a background piece of paper and the colors they want for the plate, cup, napkin, and utensils. Let them trace and cut out the shapes for their place settings. Position each piece where it belongs, paying attention to the child's right- or left-handedness. Help the children glue the pieces in place. You or the children can print or write their names on their place mats. When dry, cover with contact paper or laminate.

"Cents"-ible Shoppers

Collect newspaper grocery coupons for several weeks, then ask the children to help you cut them out. Pick out coupons for items you have on hand and place the coupons in a bag. Place the actual items on the kitchen counter or on a table within easy reach. Shake the bag and let each child draw out a coupon. Then take all the children to the "store," where they can match their coupons to the items. When everyone has had a turn, return the coupons to the bag and the food items to the table. Shake the bag and repeat.

❢ IMPORTANT SAFETY TIP:

Be sure to use child-safe scissors and supervise their use.

Play Clay

The children in your care will have hours of fun with nontoxic clay that you make yourself with this easy recipe. In a large, heavy pan, mix 3 cups flour, 3 tablespoons alum (found in the spice section of your supermarket), and $1\frac{1}{2}$ cups of salt. Add 3 tablespoons of vegetable oil and 3 cups of water. Stir constantly over medium heat until the mixture reaches the consistency of mashed potatoes. Remove from the heat and cool (be sure not to let the clay dry out). Divide into quarters and place each quarter into a clear plastic bag to protect children's skin and the kitchen counter. Make a depression in the middle of the clay in each bag and add four to six drops of food coloring. Children can help you squeeze the plastic bags to mix the color. Seal in airtight jars or heavy plastic bags when not being used.

❢ IMPORTANT SAFETY TIP:
Be sure the clay is cool before letting the children handle it.

Pretty Tissue Fish

Give each child a large outline of a fish shape to cut out. Let the children use child-safe scissors to cut half circles out of tissue paper and then glue the straight edges on the fish to create scales. Younger children may need help from you or from school-age children. Preschool and school-age children can cut out their own fish shapes. Some are certain to be creative-looking creatures!

❢ IMPORTANT SAFETY TIP:
Be sure to use child-safe scissors and supervise their use.

Your Own Ideas

Use this space to write your own fun ideas.

_____

_____

_____

_____

_____

_____

_____

_____

_____

_____

_____

_____

_____

_____

_____

_____

_____

_____

_____

_____

Chapter
3

Dining Room:
Table Toppers

C hildren will enjoy these games and crafts that need a table but aren't too messy for a room with carpeting and upholstered chairs. These activities include educational games and crafts as well as some that are just for fun! Let children use imagination and simple supplies to create their own fun or make easy, no-mess crafts. Ideas include quiet thinking games as well as low-key physical activities.

Huff and Puff!

Clear the dining room table and have half of the children stand at each side. Put five or six cotton balls about 4 inches apart down the middle of the table. The children on each side try to blow the cotton balls off the opposite side of the table. To add more fun, tell the story of the Three Little Pigs on the day you play this game.

Footsie Ball

Children love using a softly inflated beach ball in this under-the-table "sport." Divide the children into two teams. Line up each team on opposite sides of the length of the dining room table, facing each other. Have them sit on the floor and remove their shoes and socks. Then lay your dining room chairs on their sides to block off the "playing field" at each short end of the table. Let them kick the ball back and forth under the table. Everybody wins!

Food Coloring

All you need for this game are several sheets of construction paper in different colors. Have the children sit around the table with the paper in the center. Let each child choose a sheet. Have the children place the paper in front of them. Choose one for yourself and begin the game by naming your color. Then name as many foods as you can think of that are the same color. Go around the circle and let each child name foods that are the same color as his paper. Younger children will need some prompting. (NOTE: You can vary the game by letting everyone participate in naming foods for each color.)

Shopping Trip

Create a tabletop grocery store with food boxes and cans from your pantry. You'll need a toy phone, grocery bags, and play money (these supplies can be homemade). Arrange a variety of food items and a stack of grocery bags on the dining room table. Then ask the children to join you in the kitchen. Assign one or two children to go into the dining room to be grocery clerks. The others are the shoppers. Use the toy phone to call in your order. (Keep it simple so the children can remember everything.) Then have the shoppers "drive" to the store in their pretend cars. The clerks will place each order in a grocery bag and collect the play money. Take turns.

Food Sources

"Where Does This Come From?" is a game you can play using boxed, jarred, and canned food items you already have in your pantry: ketchup, pasta, tuna, milk, pickles, crackers, orange juice, green beans, pancake mix, etc. Place several unopened food items on the dining room table and ask the children to sit around the table. Start by telling the children that foods come from plants and animals. Then ask if anyone can tell you where any of the displayed items came from. (Don't be surprised if they answer, "The grocery store.") If they have trouble, point to an item such as ketchup and explain its source: "Ketchup is made from tomatoes that grow on a farm and start out as tiny seeds." The children will soon catch on and offer their own ideas.

Falling Leaves

Autumn leaves come to life in this combined art/game activity. Read a story about autumn or simply explain how leaves turn red, orange, yellow, and brown in fall. Put crayons of fall colors on the table and have the children draw simple leaf shapes to color and cut out with child-safe scissors. When they're finished, put away the art supplies and place all the leaves on top of the table. Choose one child to stay at the table while the rest sit under it. The child at the table pretends to be the wind and blows the leaves off the table. The others try to catch them as they flutter past. Give each child a turn at being the wind.

IMPORTANT SAFETY TIP:
Be sure to use child-safe scissors and supervise their use.

Night and Day

What are some things we do during the day? At night? Have fun letting children respond to your list of activities with pictures they make themselves. Give each child two pictures to color and cut out: one of the sun and one of a crescent moon. When they're finished, have everyone stay seated around the table. Make up such sentences as "You are putting on your pajamas," "You are eating lunch," and "You are dreaming." Then ask the children to respond by holding up the sun for a daytime activity or the moon for a nighttime activity. Let the children take turns making up their own day and night situations.

ᕦ IMPORTANT SAFETY TIP:

Be sure to use child-safe scissors and supervise their use.

Basketball

Children will jump and cheer when they score in this simple version of basketball. Gather a collection of soft balls (softly inflated beach balls, stuffed fabric balls, Nerf balls, etc.). Avoid balls that can hurt if thrown too hard, such as tennis balls, Ping-Pong balls, or softballs. Place a laundry basket in the middle of your table. Pull all the chairs away from the table and place the balls under the table. When you say "GO!" let everyone grab a ball and gently tap it into the air toward the basket. Everyone scrambles for balls that miss and keeps trying until all the balls are in the basket.

Eating Out

Declare a "Restaurant Day" and assign servers for each meal and snack. Furnish aprons and special hats. Tell the children what food choices you have available and help them prepare pads of paper with simple drawings of the items you are offering for each meal and snack. When the children are seated at the table, the servers use pads of paper and pencils to check off food orders from the "customers." The servers also put place settings in front of each customer and serve them the correct food. After eating in the kitchen, the wait staff clear away the customers' dishes and collect play money that the customers use to pay for their meals. Take turns at every meal and snack so everyone gets a turn at each role.

My Country

Let the children choose names for imaginary countries based on their own names. (For example, James might choose Jameslandia.) Using a library book or encyclopedia, show the children pictures of the flags of different countries and explain that each country has its own flag. Have the children create flags for their countries using paper and crayons. When they have finished coloring, use glue  or cellophane tape to attach the flags to flagpoles made from cardboard tubes. Play music with a marching tempo while the children march around the room waving their flags.

Wind Pipes

Use drinking straws to demonstrate the power of the wind. You'll need one drinking straw for each child, two pieces of construction paper in each of four colors, scissors, and cellophane tape. Let the children blow through the straws onto their hands to feel the air flow. Then have them inhale and feel the suction on their palms. Tape one piece of each color of construction paper to the top of the table. Then cut small, simple shapes from the other pieces of paper (squares, circles, triangles). Scatter these on the tabletop. Have the children blow through the straws and try to move the blue shapes onto the blue paper, the red shapes onto the red paper, etc. For a variation, have them suck on their straws until the shapes stick to the bottom of the straws; then they can release the suction so the shapes drop on the paper of a matching color.

Match Up

Take an old deck of playing cards (any kind will do: traditional playing cards or cards from an old boxed game). Cut each card in two pieces at different angles: diagonal, vertical, or horizontal. Place the card pieces facedown on a table and have the children gather around. Ask them to find two pieces that go together to make a complete card. Take turns selecting half a card from the pile, then let everybody look for their missing half. If two children choose halves of the same card, they can trade. When all the cards are back together, everyone cheers: "We matched them all up!"

Indoor Tetherball

For this activity you will need some string and a beach ball inflated to the size of a cantaloupe. Tie one end of the string to the stem of the beach ball and the other end to a table leg. The string should be long enough so the ball hangs freely but does not touch the ground and cannot reach the nearest table leg. Move dining room chairs away from the table and let the children sit on the floor around the table leg. Let them take turns tapping the ball so the string winds around the table leg and the ball touches  the leg. When a child completes this task, have him tap in the other direction until the string completely unwinds.

⚑ IMPORTANT SAFETY TIP:
Never leave children unattended with a long piece of cord or string.

Go Togethers

This matching game is fun and a little more challenging for older children. Collect an assortment of items that go together, like salt and pepper, cup and saucer, jar and lid, soap and wash cloth. Mix up the items in the middle of the table and have the children take turns finding matching sets.

Our Town

Let children build a town together using building blocks, a newspaper, and toy people, animals, and cars from your toy box. Have the children sit around the table and give each one a rectangular piece of newspaper. Put the blocks and toys in the center of the table to share. Talk about the kinds of buildings that make up a town, then have the children build whatever they want: house, apartment building, store, place of worship, hospital, supermarket, school, etc. When the buildings are complete, let the children use their imaginations to help the toy people, animals, and cars walk and drive around the town.

Season's Greetings

When a new season is coming up, talk about the season with the children seated around the table. Ask, "What do we need for summer?" See how many items the children can think of (swimming suits, sandals, sunglasses, lawn mower, picnic cooler, etc.). Make a list. Save the list and make a new one when the season changes.

Table Tennis

Clear off the top of the table and divide the children into two groups standing at opposite sides of the table. Children place their dominant hands behind their backs and use the other hand to tap a softly inflated beach ball back and forth. Teams must let the ball touch the table between taps.

Day Camp

When outdoor fun must wait for another day, take children "camping" in your dining room. Ask if any of them have *ever* been camping. Talk about the items you will need for your camp out: flashlight, blanket, play food, firewood (use building logs, wooden blocks, or unsharp-  ened pencils). Throw a blanket over the table to form a tent. Fold up one side so the children can crawl in and out. Sit inside together and use a flashlight for story time. Send children out to look for firewood, then pretend to cook a meal over the campfire.

More Bounce to the Ounce

Build good attitudes about teamwork with this easy game. Cover the table with a tablecloth and have the children sit around it. Have each child use both hands to hold the tablecloth's edges. Place a softly inflated beach ball in the middle of the table. Have the children experiment with working together to raise and lower the tablecloth so the ball soars and falls. Then see how many times they can bounce the ball without it falling to the floor.

Matching Mittens

On a winter day, have children put their mittens or gloves on the center of the dining room table. Be sure to have some extra pairs available for children who don't have any mittens with them. (If there are no mittens available, have the children make their own using child-safe scissors and construction paper of different colors.) Be sure both mittens match. Take one mitten from each pair and go into another room to hide them. Then call in the children to find their mittens. Take turns hiding the mittens.

IMPORTANT SAFETY TIP:
Be sure to use child-safe scissors and supervise their use.

Your Own Ideas

Use this space to write your own fun ideas.

Chapter
4

Living Room:
All the World's a Stage

Indoor fun includes games and activities that let children move about and stretch their imaginations. While the living room is not the place for wild, active games, it serves as a nice environment for storytelling, creative dramatics, and movement and music. Use these tips to explore emotions, create characters, burst out in song, and exercise children's minds and bodies.

Face Your Feelings

Demonstrate how your face looks when you are surprised, angry, happy, worried, scared, sleepy, helpless, etc. Then point to a child and challenge her to express an emotion that you specify. Encourage exaggeration.

Peekaboo Plates

For another way to explore emotions, have the children sit in a circle. Give each child a paper plate. Choose a child and describe an incident using a one-line scenario, such as "You wake up to find a new puppy sitting in your room." Have the child cover her face with a paper plate while she creates the expression that demonstrates her reaction. When she is ready, she lowers the plate so the other children can see how she feels. Have them imitate her look. Take turns and use a variety of emotions such as joy, surprise, excitement, apprehension, pain, and shyness.

Quiet Little Mice

Hide a "ticking" kitchen timer in the living room while the children wait in another room. Tell the children to be "quiet as mice" so they can hear the ticking. Whoever finds the timer gets to hide it for the next round. For extra fun, add "mouse whiskers" to the children's cheeks with a washable eyebrow pencil. Be sure every child gets a turn to hide the timer.

Baby Talk

Have parents send pictures of their children taken when they were babies. (Videotapes might also be fun to watch.) Spend the day talking about babies and doing baby activities. For example, have the children sit in a circle and take turns pretending to be babies who are just learning to walk or talk. At lunchtime, let them feed each other. At naptime, sing a lullaby.

Lost and Found

This modified hide-and-seek game helps children learn to trust police officers in case they ever have a problem. Talk about police officers' uniforms, name tags, and badges. Discuss whether or not you can believe people who say they are police officers but don't wear uniforms or have badges to show you. Give children examples of places to find police officers. To play the game, find something to use as a prop that will designate a "sheriff." A badge or vest (or one you make from a paper grocery bag) will serve the purpose. Make up a story about a lost child who was carrying a stuffed toy when last seen. Give one child a stuffed toy. While the sheriff covers her eyes, the children hide. The sheriff then hunts for the lost child until she finds the right one. Let the children take turns being the sheriff and the lost child.

Magnet Magic

Use cookie sheets, paper clips, and kitchen magnets to expose children to the concept of magnetism. Let two children hold the short ends of a cookie sheet with paper clips scattered on top. A third child then presses the magnet to the bottom side of the cookie sheet, moving the paper clips around without touching them. Each child will want a turn to try this one!

Swing and Sway

Encourage children to feel the beat of different kinds of music. Tune a radio to a lively station. Stop long enough to talk about how the music makes everyone feel (dreamy, jumpy, stompy). Then have everyone stand and move to the beat of the music. Change the station every minute or so. Be sure to vary the stations to include different kinds of music: rock, jazz, country, classical, etc. Let older children take turns choosing the stations.

Homemade Parade

Take everyone to the kitchen to create band instruments. Use pie tins for cymbals, shake metal measuring spoons on a ring, and hit the handles of wooden spoons together as rhythm sticks. A child can also use a wooden spoon to strike the lid of a saucepan. Be creative. Fill a margarine  tub with rice or unpopped popcorn kernels and secure the lid to make a maraca. Put on some parade music and march around the room. For extra fun, give everyone a party hat to wear. Exchange instruments so everyone gets to try them all.

❗ IMPORTANT SAFETY TIP:
   Popcorn, rice, and beans pose a choking hazard for children under age three. Omit the maracas if you have younger children in your care.

Opera House

Get a recording of an opera from the library and play part of it for the children. Explain that operas tell stories in song. Take a familiar story like the Three Little Pigs. Act as the narrator and sing the story. Then let children join in on familiar passages. Spend the rest of the day singing your conversations instead of talking. Be dramatic!

Critter Chorus

Younger children who enjoy the sounds of their own voices but aren't ready to sing a whole song enjoy this singing activity. Start by singing "Can you sing like a cow?" (Make up your own melody.) Encourage children to chime in "Moo, moo, moo." Continue the game by naming different animals.

Hoop It Up

Play a modified version of basketball using rolled-up socks for balls. Place a laundry basket on the sofa or in a large chair. Give each child two rolled-up socks. Place a strip of masking tape on the floor for a free throw line, or have children take one step away from the basket for each year they are old. Demonstrate underhand and overhand free throws. Each child attempts a first shot. If she scores, the child gets a second turn. If not, she goes to the end of the line. When everyone has had a turn, retrieve the socks and play again. Improvise other ways to shoot, such as shooting first with the right arm, then with the left, with back to the basket, with eyes closed, from a twirling position.

Props Are Tops

Give children a chance to act out seasonal activities with props you have at home. Have everyone sit in a circle on the floor. In the center, place at least a dozen items you would use for activities at different times of the year. For example, items like sunglasses, a pair of mittens, garden gloves, a toy rake, etc. Start the game by asking one child to choose a prop and act out how it is used. Then have the audience identify what she is doing and what season it is.

Pop Ups

Sit in a circle on the floor. In turn, have the children stand and name the colors they are wearing. Then make up a silly story using a lot of color words. Every time a child hears a color she is wearing, she jumps up, then sits back down. (Story example: Abigail woke up and opened her brown eyes to see a big yellow sun in the sky. She put away her gray teddy bear and took off her green pajamas.) Older children might like making up stories for younger ones to pop up for.

"Prop"-er Storytelling

Use props to involve children in a story. Get a version of the story of the Little Red Hen, such as *Not I, Not I* by Margaret Hillert (Chicago: Follett, 1981) or a Spanish version like Margot Zemach's *La Gallinita Roja: Un Viejo Cuenta* (New York: Farrar, Straus, and Giroux, 1992). Read the story to yourself to get a sense of it but don't read it to the children. "Tell" it instead. Use props like a toy shovel, play wheelbarrow, rolling pin, bread pans, etc. Be dramatic. Use a sweet voice for the little red hen and animal voices for the other animals. Assign children different roles in the story. Tell the story again, but this time when you get to each part of the story let the children pantomime the roles using the props.

Prop Ups

Let children act out a story using props you select ahead of time. Choose any story—or make up your own. Then find a selection of items you will mention in the story. For example, if the characters in the story have a dog, a clock, and a doll, find a stuffed dog, a clock, and a doll. Pass out the props to each child after you are all sitting in a circle on the floor. Then read or tell the story. Whenever you mention one of the props, the child who is holding it "pops up" to a standing position, shows his prop, then sits back down.

Upside-Down Giggles

Place pillows or cushions side by side on the floor along a wall or in front of the sofa. Have the children remove their shoes. Let them practice standing on their heads using the wall or sofa to steady their legs. Help younger ones. Get ready for giggles!

Hide and Eat

Fill clean film canisters or other small containers with snacks, such as raisins or dry cereal. "Hide" them around the room in places where little ones can easily find them. Tell the children to find their treats, and take them to the kitchen to eat. Add milk or juice for a snack.

Animal Antics

Your living room becomes a zoo in this game, which uses only a picture book of animals and the children's imagination. Ask one child to turn to any page in the book and call out the name of the animal in the picture. Then everyone follows the leader in the movements and sounds that animal makes. Everyone gets a turn being the leader. For a barnyard of fun, end the game with all the children making the movements and sounds of the animals they chose.

What's in the Bag?

Place a variety of toys in a line on the sofa. Everyone walks past and looks at all of them. Then the children sit on the floor with their backs to the sofa. While they cover their eyes, one child chooses a toy and places it in an opaque bag. She sits in front of the others. The children uncover their eyes and take turns asking questions that can be answered "yes" or "no." For example: "Is the toy red?" "Does it squeak?" The first child to correctly guess which toy is in the bag selects the toy for the next round. Be sure everyone gets a turn.

Jack and Jill

Recite the poem "Jack and Jill." Have children lie on the floor and roll the length of the room. Let them try it with arms outstretched and with arms pulled in front of their bodies. For extra fun, let them take turns carrying a clean, empty bucket to one end of the room and filling it at a pretend well. Have them act as if the bucket is heavy, drop it, and then roll across the room.

Prompts and Circumstance

Using songs or poems the children already know, start by singing or reciting the entire work together. Then lead off the song or poem again with the first few words of each line. Pause and put your hand to your ear to indicate that the children should finish the line. Take turns being the leader.

Acting Out

Play a recording of a familiar story and have children act it out. Rather than assigning roles, let everyone stand in a circle and act out every part together as the narrator on the recording reads. Gallop on a horse, flap like a bird, waddle like a penguin—whatever the story suggests.

Pick a Part

Let children act out silly experiences. Beforehand, write a number of ideas on slips of paper: "You have gum stuck to your shoe," "You are swimming through a pool full of chocolate pudding," "You have tickle bugs under your clothes," "You are walking on a very hot sidewalk." Be creative and outrageous, but avoid anything scary like ghosts or monsters. Place the slips of paper in a box or other container and have the children take turns picking the part they'll act out. For extra fun, let them act out silly experiences and have the audience guess what the actors are doing.

Fire Escape

Teach fire safety with this dramatic activity. Talk about fire and what to do if a house is on fire, stressing the escape routes you have planned from each room. Talk about crawling on the floor to stay under heavy smoke and show children how to check a door for heat by using the backs of their hands. Teach them that a hot door should not be opened. Act out the "Stop, Drop, and Roll" technique to use if clothes are on fire. (Stop where you are. Drop to the floor. Roll over and over to smother the flames.) Next, use a piece of yellow construction paper cut out to look like flames. Attach a loop of masking tape to the back so you can stick it onto surfaces. Place it somewhere in the room and yell "FIRE!" Have the children yell with you. Then watch to see if they know what to do. Point out the correct behavior and repeat the "performance." When everyone is reassembled in the living room, stick the "fire" onto one of the children's shirts. Say, "Your clothes are on fire!" Watch to see what the child does. If necessary yell, "Stop, Drop, and Roll!"

A Ticket to Ride

Line up chairs behind each other. Sit in the first chair and use a lid to a large pan as a steering wheel. Fasten your imaginary seat belt. Tell the children to get on the bus. When they have fastened their own imaginary seat belts, announce your destination: Alaska, an amusement park, a rain forest, a playground, the zoo. As you "drive," have the children shout out the things they "see": penguins, snow, a merry-go-round, banana trees, a swing, monkeys. Take turns being the driver and selecting the destinations.

Picture This

From old magazines, cut out pictures of scenes with people in them. The people should be a variety of ages, sizes, cultures, abilities, classes, etc. Some good magazines to use include *Life, National Geographic,* and *Smithsonian.* Sit with children in a circle on the floor and place several pictures in the center. Let the children choose pictures and make up stories about them. Allow plenty of thinking time. Start with your own choice to give the children an example. Then let them take turns. They may make up a whole story or just describe what they see. Ask them how they think the people in the picture feel and why they might feel that way. Younger children may just say "pretty," "puppy," or "mommy," and that's fine.

Story Detectives

Choose five or six storybooks you have read to the children many times. Have the children sit on the floor in a circle. Place the books in the center. Recite one or two sentences from one of the books. Take turns letting each child guess which book the sentence came from. Give the same child several clues until she guesses it, or go around the circle, adding a new clue when you get to the next child. Older children will enjoy giving clues.

Sharing Favorite Stories

Ask parents to bring their child's favorite picture book or storybook from home (be sure the child's name is in it). Save these for an "inside" day. At various times during the day, say: "Drop everything and read!" Stop whatever you're doing and go to the living room for a story. Put all the books in a pile and choose one with your eyes closed. The child who brought the book gets to sit on your lap while you read the story to the group. After the story, ask the child why it's her favorite. Ask if anyone else has heard that story. Stop for several story breaks during the day. Remove books you've already read from the pile so that all will be read.

Who or What?

Sit together in a circle with one person (the "actor") standing in the middle. If you go first, the children will understand what to do. The actor in the middle acts out a "person" or "thing" while the audience tries to guess who or what it is. Examples: swimmer, hula dancer, cowboy riding a horse, a tree in the wind, a tornado. Younger children may need prompting, so be prepared to whisper an idea or two.

Colorful Cleanup

Give each child a paper grocery bag with a different color of construction paper taped or stapled to the outside. Scatter toys of different color around the room or use toys already on the floor. Have the children pick up the toys matching the color on their bags. When everything is in the bags, dump the toys out again and exchange bags.

Squeal and Scatter

Choose one child to be the "squealer." Place one piece of newspaper for each of the other children somewhere on the floor—but no newspaper for the "squealer." The children crawl around the room like kittens. The squealer squeals and sits on a piece of newspaper. The kittens jump up and run to sit on the other pieces. The child left without a place to sit squeals for the next round.

Prowling for Peanuts

Blindfold the children and scatter unshelled peanuts on the floor. (NOTE: If a child is afraid of the blindfold, have her close her eyes tightly instead.) Say "GO!" and everyone crawls around, trying to find the peanuts. Play as a group or one at a time, giving hints like "You're real close," "A little to the right," "Behind you." When all peanuts are found, take them into the kitchen and make peanut butter: Remove shells and place in blender with a dab of vegetable oil. Use the peanut butter for a snack or lunch. Refrigerate any leftover peanut butter.

Your Own Ideas

Use this space to write your own fun ideas.

Chapter

5

Bed and Bath:
Imagination Stations

Because you probably don't use the bedroom for child care—or use it only for naptime—it's a great place for something new to do on a rainy or snowy day. Use the bedroom for quiet activities like imaginative games, puppets, storytelling, and playing soft music. That way, the children will continue to regard the room as a place for rest and comfort. You probably never thought of the bathroom as a play area, either. But a bad weather day calls for creativity. You'll be surprised how much fun you can have in this room. Just be sure to remove all hair dryers, curling irons, electric razors, and other electrical appliances from the bathroom before children play there. And carefully supervise activities using water in the sink or tub.

Bedroom: Daydreams and Lullabies

Let children dream the day away using their imagination, creativity, and problem solving skills. These quiet activities include drama, movement and music, learning, and lots of fun.

When You Were a Baby

Talk about how babies love to hear lullabies while they are being rocked. Take turns wrapping each child in his naptime blanket while he holds a comfort toy. Rock each child like a baby while you sing or play recordings of different lullabies. Your library may have books or recordings in their children's collection. Look for *The Lullaby Songbook*, edited by Jane Yolen (San Diego: Harcourt, Brace, Jovanovich, 1986), Jenny Wood's *First Songs & Action Rhymes* (New York: First Aladdin Books, 1991), or *The Nursery Treasury*, edited by Sally Emerson (New York: Doubleday, 1988). Let each child choose his favorite song. This is a comforting game for a cold or stormy day.

Tender Tootsies

Have the children remove their shoes and socks and sit on the edge of the bed with their feet hanging over the sides. Start the game by saying "I feel pudding (or a hot sidewalk, or fish nibbling) on my feet." Let the children pretend they feel the same thing. Then take turns letting each child imagine something new.

Emergency!

Remove shoes and sit in a semicircle on the bed. Unplug your phone and bring it with you onto the bed. Explain that dialing 911 is a way to get help in an emergency. Then demonstrate how to dial 911. Let each child practice pushing the buttons. Let each child give a reason to call for help.

Tender Tots

Have each child bring a doll or stuffed animal and a blanket from home. Allow children to share a toy doctor kit. Let each child make up a story about what happened to his patient, lay the toy on the bed, and treat the ailment using tools from the doctor kit. Talk about tenderness, comfort, and healing.

Rhythm Section

Have children remove their shoes. Then sit in a circle on the bed. Take turns creating rhythms by clapping, snapping, and tapping. Try to repeat each child's sounds.

Here Comes Freddy Feather!

Children remove their shoes and socks and lie on the bed. They can cover up with their naptime blankets but leave their feet sticking out. Have them close their eyes, then say "Here comes Freddy Feather. Who will he tickle next?" Lightly brush a feather across someone's feet. Wait until the giggling stops before going to the next child. Give everyone a turn at being Freddy Feather. Be sure to give only a light brush with the feather. No excessive tickling.

The Nose Knows

In another room, spray a cotton ball with cologne and let everyone smell it. While the children wait in the hall, hide the cotton ball in the bedroom. Let the children enter the bedroom and sniff until someone finds the cotton ball. The one who finds it gets to hide it next.

Recording Artists

Teach children several lullabies, then use a tape recorder while they sing together. Have them wrap their favorite doll or stuffed animal in a blanket. Play the recording while they rock their toys to sleep.

Touch and Tell

Explore the sense of touch by selecting objects in the bedroom and describing how they feel. For example, the pillow is soft, the headboard is hard. Call out a texture and have children touch something in the room that has that texture. Use a variety of textures, such as rough, smooth, sandy, scratchy, lumpy.

Undercover

Select pairs of toys from your toy collection: two dolls, two balls, two cars, two books, etc. Place one of each set into a paper grocery bag. Have the children remove their shoes and sit in a circle on the bed. Place a baby blanket in the middle of the circle. Now place the other toys from the sets around the border of the blanket. While the children cover their eyes,

place one toy from the bag under the blanket. Let the children uncover their eyes and try to guess which of the visible toys matches the one that's hidden. Let everyone have a turn to guess.

The Queen Has Lost Her Sparkles

Use your own inexpensive costume jewelry or collect some from garage sales and save it for a rainy day. Display the jewelry on the bed and let the children examine it. Make up a story about mischievous elves who hide the queen's sparkles while she sleeps. While the children wait in the hall, hide the pieces of jewelry in easy-to-find places in the room. When the children return, ask them to help the queen find her sparkles. After the search, help the children try on what they found.

❗ IMPORTANT SAFETY TIP:

Beads and small earrings can be a choking hazard. Keep them away from children under age three.

Sock Talk

Children put socks on their hands to create sock puppets. Demonstrate how to move their hands to simulate puppets talking to each other. Make up a silly conversation and let the children join in. For extra fun, attach clip-on earrings to the socks for sparkling eyes.

Leaping in the Light

Children duck down beside one side of the bed while you duck down beside the opposite side. With a flashlight, try to "catch" children in the spotlight as they pop up and down sporadically. Take turns with the flashlight.

A New View

Give children a view of your neighborhood that is different from the one they usually see. Pull back your bedroom curtains and let the children view your neighborhood. Ask them to describe what they see and what it could mean. For example, if they see a swing set in a neighbor's yard, the family may have children. Talk about their observations.

Parts Department

Children stand in front of the mirror and point to parts of their body. Begin with heads, arms, legs, and tummies. Proceed to smaller features: wrists, knees, fingernails, eyebrows, etc. Talk about ways people are alike and different. Features such as hair color and height make people unique.

All-Weather Clothes

With the children sitting together on the bed, talk about dressing for the day's weather. Ask children what they need to wear to be comfortable. Take turns having each child add an item to the list: long underwear, boots, raincoat, umbrella, snow pants, etc. Talk about layering clothing for extra warmth.

Handy Hands

With everyone sitting together on the bed, the children take turns demonstrating what they can do with their hands: clap, tie a shoe, hold a toy, throw a ball, etc. Prompt additional ideas by asking how they will use their hands when they grow up: drive a car, diaper a baby, type a letter, play a piano, etc.

Beltway

Children stand around the edges of the bed. Place several soft belts on the bed and let children manipulate them into simple objects and shapes: snakes, circles, letters of the alphabet, etc. Perhaps they'd like to work as a group to make a cooperative design using all the belts at once.

Tools of the Trade

Have children imagine themselves in different career roles. Then ask them to list the items they'd need to perform those jobs. For example, a firefighter needs a fire truck, hose, ladder, coat, etc. Ask what they'd need to be an astronaut, ballet dancer, doctor, teacher, etc. What would they like and not like about those jobs?

Now Hear This!

Have children cover their eyes while you make a sound using something in the room: raise blinds, open and shut a drawer, turn a lamp on and off, slide the closet door. Children take turns guessing what made the sound. Then take turns creating sounds for others to guess.

Silly Sentences

Choose a letter of the alphabet and make up a silly sentence using as many words as you can that begin with that sound. Example: Bailey is beside the blue bedspread balancing on a ball. Choose another letter and let children help you make up another silly sentence.

Puzzle Solvers

Bring in two or three wooden puzzles and place them on the edge of the bed. While children cover their eyes, lay all the pieces on surfaces around the room. Let the children find the pieces, then work together to complete all of the puzzles.

Snowball Fun

Divide the group on each side of the bed. Open an inexpensive bag of cotton balls and give half to each side. Have the children pop up and down and toss cotton balls at each other.

Count on This

Take turns naming an object in the room. Then together everyone counts how many like items there are in the room. How many lamps? How many noses? How many pillows? Touch each item so that the children know exactly what they're counting.

Windy Weather

Cut a leaf shape out of a piece of tissue paper or other lightweight paper. Place it on the center of the bed. Have half of the group of children stand on each side of the bed. When you say "GO!" children blow as hard as they can until one team blows the leaf off the other team's side. Change teams around and play enough times that everyone "wins." Talk about the power of the wind to blow leaves around.

Weather Wearables

Put a variety of items from the bedroom and closet onto the bed (belt, earrings, sunglasses, necktie, sweater, etc.). Ask children questions about items they might need in different kinds of weather. Which would you need on a cold day? Which on a hot day? Ask questions one at a time. Add or take away items for the next round. After everyone has had a turn, let children make up questions.

Word Calls

This naming game helps increase children's vocabulary. Point to an item in the room and ask, "What do you call this?" For example, point to your dresser. Let the children name the item. Then give them alternative words for the same item (bureau, chest of drawers). Some examples: rug/carpet, curtains/drapes, purse/pocketbook, mirror/looking glass.

Listen and Do

Even younger children who can't talk yet enjoy this game. Take turns giving each child a command (from simple to difficult, depending on the child's age). Examples: "Samuel, can you walk over and touch the door?" "Elizabeth, can you touch all the furniture in the room that is taller than you?" Encourage each performer with a round of applause.

Bathroom: Health and Beauty Duty

Water play and personal hygiene activities include fun with bubbles, art projects, and lessons in good grooming. Be sure to remove electrical appliances from the room. And never leave children unattended around any water source—even a few inches of water in a tub.

Bathtub Art

Tape two large pieces of paper on the far wall of the tub enclosure and lay towels or rubber mats in the bottom of the tub to prevent slipping. Have the children remove socks and shoes and wear smocks. Have two children sit (not stand) on the edge of the tub facing the paper. Let each child paint a picture. When the first two children are finished, move their pictures higher on the wall to dry. Tape new paper for the next two painters. For easy cleanup, use washable paints so you can use the tap to wash children's hands. And when the pictures are dry, use the shower spray to clean the wall.

Shine Your Machine

Talk to children about their bodies and how to keep themselves clean. Tell them their hands are their food retrievers and teach proper hand washing. Tell them their teeth are their grinders and demonstrate proper brushing. And tell them their hair is their crown. Teach them how to comb or brush their hair.

Illustration from *Those Icky Sticky Smelly Cavity-Causing but...Invisible Germs*, Judith Rice (St. Paul, MN: Redleaf Press, 1997).

Target Practice

Bring in several pans of snow from outside and dump into the bathtub. Tape a piece of bright paper to the wall. Everyone puts on mittens, makes snowballs, and throws them at the target. Easy cleanup: What's left melts away!

Close Shaves

Draw a picture of a man's face on a heavy paper grocery bag and tape it to the bathroom countertop. Squirt shaving cream on the face's beard and moustache area. Take turns using Popsicle sticks to shave the face. What happens if you leave part of the face unshaven? Demonstrate which areas to leave alone if someone wants a pencil-thin moustache, a goatee, or sideburns. Rinse sticks with water.

Bubble Up

How many bubbles does it take to fill the sink or bathtub if everyone blows bubbles at once? Give everyone a straw and an empty margarine tub with a lid. Cut two holes on opposite sides of the lid. One hole is for the straw. The other is for bubbles to come out. Pour $\frac{1}{2}$ cup of water and a few drops of dish soap in each margarine tub and put on the lids. Show the children how to blow through the straw. Then insert straws in lids. Have the children lean over the sink or tub and blow. Bubbles cascade down the side of the margarine tub in a long chain.

IMPORTANT SAFETY TIP:

Be sure children know how to blow through the straws so they don't suck the bubble solution into their mouths.

Sink or Swim

Run several inches of water into the tub and have the children bring you a variety of waterproof items such as a ball, metal car, comb, clothespin, or section of train track. Ask which items children think will float and which will sink. Then try the items one at a time.

IMPORTANT SAFETY TIP:

Never leave children unattended near any water source.

Car Wash

Use colored chalk to draw a large car on the tile wall of the tub enclosure. Give each child a clean squeeze bottle (such as the kind dish soap or mustard comes in). Fill the bottles with water from the tap. Everyone stands at the edge of the tub. When you say "GO!" the children squirt water onto the car until it is so "clean" that it disappears.

Scrambled Bubbles

Fill a clean sink with 3 inches of warm water and a few drops of dish soap. Beat with a manual eggbeater or whisk until suds form. Everyone gets a turn. Skim off some of the bubbles if the sink gets too full of suds.

IMPORTANT SAFETY TIP:
Do NOT use an electric mixer for this activity.

Bathroom Manners

Talk about what a bathroom is used for: brushing teeth, bathing, using the toilet, washing hands, combing hair, etc. Now walk through each task in sequence. For example, to take a bath, what do you do first? Second? Third? Fill the tub, get a towel, bathe, dry off, let out the water, hang up towel. Teach the children to flush the toilet, wash their hands, clean toothpaste out of the sink, hang up towels, and respect others' privacy by always knocking on the door. Children will gain independence and self-confidence.

Boats Afloat

Make small "boats" out of plastic caps from 1-gallon milk jugs. Cut colored paper into triangles to make sails. Then glue the sails into place across the diameter of each cap's interior. Use a different color for each child's sail. Each child gets a drinking straw. Fill a clean sink with 2 or 3 inches of water and set the boats to sail. Children use the straws to blow on their sails in order to maneuver their boats across the water.

What Could It Be?

Wash and dry the sink and put in the stopper. Bring in a variety of small toys. Show the toys to the children and set the toys on the vanity. Select one toy and place it in the sink. Have a child stand in front of the sink so he can reach into the sink but cannot see into it. (If a child is too tall, have him bend his knees or kneel on a stool.) The child feels the toy and tries to guess what it is. Everyone gets a turn.

Fill 'er Up

Give each child a clean plastic squeeze bottle filled with water. Place a variety of lidless plastic containers in a clean, dry tub. Children stand next to the tub. When you say "GO!" the children aim at the targets, trying to fill them with water. (This isn't as easy as it sounds!) Refill squeeze bottles as needed.

Super Suds

For extra big bubbles, have the children use the cardboard tube from an empty roll of bathroom tissue instead of a traditional bubble wand. Fill a large plastic bowl with a bubble mixture. (Make your own by mixing $1/2$ gallon water with $1/4$ cup liquid dish soap.) Set the bowl in the tub. Children kneel at the edge of the tub and dip one end of the tube into the mixture. Then they cover their mouths with the dry end and blow extra big bubbles into the tub enclosure.

Your Own Ideas

Use this space to write your own fun ideas.

_____

_____

_____

_____

_____

_____

_____

_____

_____

_____

_____

_____

_____

_____

_____

_____

_____

_____

_____

_____

_____

_____

_____

_____

6

Garage:
Action Heroes

A ctive movement is the key element in these games and crafts for the garage. If it's cold, have children wear their coats and it will almost seem as if you're all the way outside! Before the children come for the day, back out the car and be sure your garage is child safe, with tools, hazardous chemicals, and other dangerous items locked out of reach.

Mini Folks

Bring pans of snow into the garage and let the children make miniature snowpeople on the garage floor. Move the completed snowpeople outside to greet the children's parents at the end of the day.

Winter in July

With snow brought into the garage from outside, have the children make a dozen or more clean snowballs. Pop a few in the freezer to save until summer.

Hop, Skip, and Jump

Children take turns shouting an active word, like "hop," "jump," "spin." Everyone performs that movement.

Bubble Blowout

Blowing bubbles is extra fun when you do it in the "off" season. For summer fun in fall or winter, lay a plastic cloth on the garage floor. Have the children sit on the outer edges of the cloth. Then put your favorite bubble-blowing solution in a plastic bowl or mug. Children can use plastic bubble wands, but other items make for extra fun. Try using empty thread spools, cardboard tubes from bathroom tissue, or wands cut from the side of a plastic

milk jug. (First cut a flat side from the jug. Then draw a wand and cut it out. You can get two wands from each flat side.)

❗ IMPORTANT SAFETY TIP:

The floor may be slippery, or children may have bubble soap on their shoes. Remind everyone to walk slowly and carefully when this activity is over.

Up, Up, and Away

Pair off the children according to age. Give each pair a bath towel and a softly inflated beach ball or Nerf ball. While the children grasp a corner of the towel in each hand, place a ball in the center. They bounce the ball into the air and catch it without letting the ball fall to the floor. For a fun variation, give each child a plastic or stiff paper plate and a ball. Children hold the plate waist high and use it as a paddle to tap the ball into the air, let it fall, and tap it again.

Three-Ring Circus

Use chalk to draw simple animal shapes in three big circles on the floor. Space the drawings so the children can step from one to another. You can draw more animals than the number of children in the group, but be sure to have at least one for each child. Children walk around the outside of a circle until you say "STOP!" Then they step inside the nearest animal shape. Children take turns going to the center of the circles to act like the animals they're standing on. Repeat until everyone has had a turn. Switch circles.

Scramble!

Draw chalk circles on the garage floor, but draw one less than the number of children in your group. Everyone walks around the garage while you clap and sing a favorite song. When you suddenly stop singing in the middle of a verse, children scramble to stand in a circle. The child left without a circle stands next to you as your helper and claps during the next round. Before starting the next round, let the child who is your newest helper erase one circle with the toe of her shoe or a rag.

Peanut Parade

Line up a row of empty plastic bowls about 1 foot apart at one end of the garage. Place a bag of packing "peanuts" at the other end. Children scoop the peanuts with a serving spoon and carry them across the floor to fill their bowls. Balance is important because the lightweight packing material flies off the spoons if the children run too fast.

♀ IMPORTANT SAFETY TIP:
Packing peanuts can be a choking hazard. Supervise this activity and be sure all pieces are picked up when the activity is over.

Tap! Tap! Tap!

Turn your garage into a construction site with scrap lumber, large-headed nails, and a hammer for each child (ask parents to bring one and be sure the hammers are labeled with the children's names). Lay a piece of lumber on the floor for each child. Start a nail in each piece by tapping it once or twice so no one has to hold the nail. Children can hold the hammer with both hands and pound away. Be sure you have plenty of nails for extra turns.

IMPORTANT SAFETY TIP:

To prevent splinters, sand any rough edges on the wood before letting the children handle the pieces.

Hoop Dreams

Place a laundry basket on a chair, stool, or table about 3 feet off the floor. Children take turns trying to score, using a softball, beach ball, or basketball.

Flying Saucers

Use paper plates as unidentified flying objects. Children stand on one side of the garage and fling paper plates with the wrist movements used to throw Frisbees. When all aliens have landed, everyone runs to the landing site and throws the plates in the opposite direction. Help the younger children learn the wrist motion. For extra fun, have children color their spaceships with crayons before blast off.

IMPORTANT SAFETY TIP:

To avoid eye injury from flying plates, be sure all children are on the same side of the garage before each blast off.

Footprint Fun

Lay a 4- to 6-foot piece of butcher paper or leftover wallpaper (use the unprinted side) on the floor and have the children remove their shoes and socks. Pour thin layers of tempera paint into clean trays, using a different color for each child. Place the tray at the edge of one end of the paper. As they take turns stepping into the paint, then onto the paper, hold each child's hand.

Continue holding their hands as the children walk the length of the paper, being careful not to step on anyone else's footprints. When a child gets to the end, wash her feet in a plastic dishpan full of warm, soapy water, and dry. Start half the children at each end of the paper so you'll have as many light and dark footprints at the top and bottom. Let the paper dry and exhibit it for parents to enjoy. For extra fun, make another picture using handprints.

Tumbling Tower

Children build a tall tower using clean, empty containers with lids (for example, potato chip canisters, margarine tubs, or ice cream cartons). Encourage cooperation and suggest putting the larger cans on the bottom for better support. Take turns knocking the tower down.

Spare Time

Place ten empty plastic soft drink bottles in a straight line at one end of the garage. Children take turns rolling a ball toward the bottles trying to knock down a "pin" or two. Place the bottles in a line rather than in the traditional bowling triangle pattern. This adds a team feeling to the game because it takes several children to knock down all the bottles.

Ring Toss

Fill several plastic soft drink bottles with water. Cap lids tightly. Place bottles in a random pattern on the floor. Cut out the centers of paper plates so the paper rings fit easily over the necks of the bottles. (Children can use child-safe scissors to help with this task.) Give everyone three or four rings. Stick a piece of masking tape on the floor. Children stand behind the line and toss the rings, trying to make the rings encircle the bottles.

Get Your Kicks

Lay two laundry baskets or large empty boxes on their sides on opposite ends of the floor. Using a beach ball or other large, soft ball, have the children tap the ball with the sides of their feet. Everyone is on the same team, working together to get the ball into the basket or box.

Yellow Brick Road

Use chalk to draw a hopscotch pattern on the floor. Alternate one square, two squares, one square, two squares, as the pattern curves like a snake and connects back to its starting point. Show the children how to hop from one foot to two feet. Space the children so no one jumps on anyone else's heels. When you say "GO!" children start around the pattern, using one foot or two feet as the pattern indicates. Say "STOP!" and everyone freezes. Say "TURN AROUND!" and everyone turns and continues in the opposite direction. For extra fun, try the game with the children jumping on single squares with feet together and on double squares with feet apart (like jumping jacks). Younger children may have difficulty with the footwork, so encourage them to hop any way they can.

Roll Away

Use chalk to draw a circle with a 3-foot diameter in the center of the floor. Children form another circle by backing up as far as the walls allow. Take turns rolling a beach ball so that it comes to rest inside the chalk circle. Make a chalk tally mark on the floor each time someone succeeds. When the group gets to ten, erase the chalk circle and draw a new, smaller one. For extra fun and a little more challenge for older children, use a hula hoop instead of the chalk circle. Children will have to roll the ball a little harder.

Silly Shape-Up

Bring a tape, compact disc, or record player into the garage. Everyone stands in a circle while you lead exercises to the beat of lively music. Do jumping jacks, toe touches, and hop around. Silly movements are welcome. Let the children take turns leading the group.

Ladder Patter

Lay a ladder flat on the floor. Children take turns walking the length of the ladder, stepping on the floor between the rungs. (Hold the younger children's hands.) When this is no longer a challenge, try walking sideways, crossing one foot over the other.

❢ IMPORTANT SAFETY TIP:

To avoid falls, be sure children walk only BETWEEN the rungs of the ladder, not on the ladder itself.

Tightrope Walker

Draw a chalk line the length of the floor. Open an umbrella and demonstrate how a high-wire acrobat walks with only an umbrella to help her balance. Ham it up! Encourage the "audience" to ooh and ahh as if they're at the circus. Everyone gets a turn to walk the tightrope using the umbrella. If you have a recording of lively circus music, play it during each child's walk.

Bag It

Divide the children into two groups. Give each child in the first group a paper grocery bag with the sides rolled down twice to create a sturdy rim. Give each child in the second group a pair of socks that have been rolled into a ball. When you say "GO!" the children with sock balls toss them in the air. The others try to catch them in the bags. Toss the sock balls three times, then switch groups.

Fresh Paint!

Assemble a collection of riding toys like cars, wagons, and scooters. Park each one on a separate square of newspaper. Give each child a small container of water and a paint brush and let them "paint" their riding toys.

Your Own Ideas

Use this space to write your own fun ideas.

Chapter

7

The Room in Your Heart:
Caring and Sharing

C aring and sharing life skills, sensitivity toward people with disabilities, and gift giving are the themes of these activities. This chapter also provides suggestions for modeling and encouraging loving behavior.

Thoughtful Acts

Gift Givers

Children practice the art of giving in this imaginary gift-giving activity. Have them sit together and take turns telling about what they like and activities they enjoy. (For example, JoAnn really likes art projects; Jonathan loves animals.) Pretend the children can give each other the most wonderful gifts selected just for that person. What would the gifts be? Go around the room and have the children tell each other the gifts they'd like to give.

Grandparents' Day

Grandparents are often curious about their grandchildren's child care. Take turns inviting them to spend a morning with you. Let them observe a typical day by planning routine activities. If a grandparent offers to read a story or help with an art project, accept the help. Everyone will benefit from the experience.

Look What's New!

Children may want to bring a new brother or sister, a new pet, or even a new toy to show their friends. Provide time for sharing at the start or end of the day. (Babies and puppies go home with the parent and don't spend the day with you!)

Dinner at the White House

Demonstrate the use of good manners. On index cards, write cues to good table manners: using napkins, keeping elbows off the table, chewing with mouth closed, excusing oneself from the table, saying please and thank you, covering a cough, sneeze, or yawn, etc. Provide all the props. Turn over one card at a time and point to the child who will then model the correct behavior. When everyone knows proper etiquette, pretend you are dining at the White House. Let children wear play dress-up clothes for lunch. Set flowers on the table, lower the lights, and play classical music to set the mood. Use low voices for polite conversation. You'll be pleased with the children's behavior. For extra fun, invite parents for a potluck dinner so the children can show off their new manners.

Picky Eaters

If a parent tells you a child is a picky eater, note which foods you prepare that the child likes. (Children are often less particular in child care than at home.) Share your recipes with the parent in a positive way, such as, "Abigail loves my macaroni and cheese when I put tuna in it, and she really loves buttered carrots." Parents will like knowing what they can fix at home that their children will eat.

Many Cultures

If you have friends from other countries, ask them to stop in to meet the children and to share stories of their homelands. Have the children find out where their ancestors came from. Share stories and information about each child's family history. Get a wall map and place a star on each country the children mention. Teach children that the world is filled with people of many different cultures. Select library books and videotapes that depict a variety of people.

Meals on Wheels

Most child care parents get acquainted, and some even become friends. If this is true in your situation, you can start a welcome chain of meals at the home of one of your child care families who has a new baby, an illness, or a family emergency. Ask the other families to sign up for an evening when they will take a casserole or a carryout meal to the family who needs help.

Emergency Care

If one of your family child care parents has an emergency, offer to keep their child overnight. Because the child is used to sleeping, eating, and playing in your home, he'll fare much better than with a neighbor he hardly knows.

The Happy Face Jar

Cut construction paper into 2-by-4-inch strips. Use a different color for each child. Whenever you notice a child behaving in a polite or caring way, jot down your observation on a piece of paper of that child's color. Collect the papers in a clear jar with a happy face on the front. (Make the happy face from a circle of construction paper. Draw the face with a marker. Tape to the jar.) Be sure each child has several reports in the jar by the end of the week. On Friday send them home to share with parents. Parents love reading good reports on their children, and you'll notice an increase in positive behavior during the day.

Baby School

Toddlers love babies but need help learning how to act toward them. Hold a session of "baby school." Give each child a doll for the lessons. Show them how to stroke a baby's arm, support a baby's head, kiss the baby only on the top of the head, and how to speak softly. Praise the children's efforts.

Corny Cards

Make a corny greeting card for fathers, using popped and unpopped kernels of corn. You'll need popcorn, construction paper, a marker, scissors, and glue. Fold a piece of construction paper in half to make the greeting card. Use a marker to draw a corncob shape about 5 inches long in the middle of a piece of construction paper. Give the children corn kernels to glue onto the shape. Cut strips of green construction paper about 4 inches long. Have the children glue two strips onto the paper so they look like a corn husk. Then draw several curved lines away from the ear and let children glue popped corn at the end of the curves. Inside the card, write "You're the Best POP Ever!" and the child's name. Older children can write or print the message and sign the cards themselves. Save the unused corn for future projects.

⁝ IMPORTANT SAFETY TIP:
Items used in this craft are too small for children under age three.

My Mommy! My Daddy!

When parents pick up their children at the end of the day, give them a minute or two alone without the other children crowding around. When you see a parent in the doorway, take everyone else to another room to play. The parent and child can greet each other and ask about each other's day. You can then return to say your good-byes.

Thank-You Notes

Parents put a lot of trust in you to care for their children, and you get attached to the children in your care. Write personal notes to each parent thanking them for sharing their children with you. Parents will treasure your note.

Kiddy Calls

If parents can receive personal calls at work, ask their permission to let their children call. (Ask what time is most convenient.) If the parent can't be reached, ask for the number of a grandparent, aunt, uncle, or close friend. Take turns letting one child make a call each day.

Warm-Ups

In the dead of winter, a little extra warmth is welcome. So send children home in extra warm coats. About ten minutes before parents are due, toss all the coats and baby blankets in your dryer to warm them up. Take them out when it's time to go home.

Referral Reward

Before you advertise a child care opening, offer a $10 reward to any parent who refers a friend who enrolls a child.

Sensitivity Training

Like many adults, most children are unfamiliar with people who have disabilities. Tell the children that some people are born with differing abilities and that some differences result from accidents or disease. Talk about ways disabilities make routine tasks difficult, but emphasize the things that people are able to do, rather than the things they cannot.

Teach the children that people who are challenged want to be treated like everyone else. Tell the children not to stare but not to ignore people with disabilities, either. Talk about the ways people are alike. Teach the children not to assume that a person with a disability needs help but to ask "Do you need help?" or "How can I help you?"

Contact local agencies that may be willing to lend equipment such as braille cards, hearing aids, braces, or wheelchairs that you can use to enhance your lessons. The videotape *The Same Inside* is available from the March of Dimes Birth Defects Foundation. (Contact the Program Services Department at 1275 Mamaroneck Avenue, White Plains, NY 10605, 914-428-7100, or call your local March of Dimes chapter.)

Role Model

Choose a child to sit on a chair and pretend to be unable to walk. (If possible, borrow a wheelchair for this activity.) With the other children's help, act out ways people might react: ignoring, staring, being afraid, teasing, being too "nice," such as patting him on the head. Then ask the child sitting in the chair how it feels to be treated those ways. Demonstrate treating the child the same way you'd treat a child who can walk.

❗ IMPORTANT SAFETY TIP:
Be sure to keep wheelchair away from stairs.

Close Your Eyes

Use scarves to cover the children's eyes. (If a child is hesitant or afraid of the blindfold, have her close her eyes tightly.) Move to the other side of the room and ask them, one at a time, to walk toward the sound of your voice. Talk about ways they can move around if they can't see. Explain that some people use guide dogs to help them. These are working dogs and should not be petted while they are assisting someone.

❗ IMPORTANT SAFETY TIP:
To avoid falls, be sure to move loose rugs or furniture that a blindfolded child could trip over.

Touch and Tell

Explain that people with vision or hearing challenges rely on other senses. Blindfold the children or have them close their eyes tightly. Hand them a variety of objects: cotton ball, spoon, pencil, etc. Have them tell you what the items are. Include a variety of fruits, and encourage them to use their sense of smell as well as touch.

Code Words

Talk about the way people with vision impairments read using braille. Show the children braille books or cards and let them feel the bumps. Ask them if they have noticed braille words on signs in public places like elevator buttons and pay phones.

Signs of the Times

Talk about the ways hearing people use gestures in everyday speech. Explain that some people with hearing impairments use a language of gestures. Using a simple sign language book from the library, teach children some basic signs for phrases like "I love you" and "My name is..." Practice together. Look for *Sign Language ABC* by Linda Bove (New York: Children's Television Workshop, 1985) or *Handtalk:*

An ABC of Finger Spelling and Sign Language by Remy Charlip, Mary Beth, and George Ancona (New York: Aladdin Books, 1986).

Lip Reading

Have the children sit in a circle while you mouth the words to a simple song or give instructions such as "stand up." See if the children can figure out what you're trying to say without being able to hear you.

Hearing Aid

Talk about the ways that hearing aids help people with hearing impairments. Then use a cardboard tube from an empty roll of wrapping paper to demonstrate what a hearing aid does. Have the children take turns sitting in the center of a circle with the tube. While the child holds the tube to one ear, whisper a sentence like "We're having tomato soup for lunch" into one end of the tube. Have the child repeat the sentence.

Feel the Beat

Talk about the ways that a person who can't hear may rely on vibrations to "hear." Have the children lie on the floor while you stomp around them using different rhythms. Ask them to feel the vibrations. If you have a pager that vibrates, call the telephone number and let the children feel it "ring." Talk about other ways to signal to a person who can't hear, such as using a flashing light instead of a chime to indicate that someone is ringing the doorbell.

Hands On

Have the children hold one arm behind their backs and try to perform tasks they usually do with two hands: tie a shoe, open a jar, etc. Or have the children wear mittens and try to button their sweaters. Talk about how these tasks take longer and require more concentration but can still be accomplished by people who either do not have or cannot use their hands.

Gifts from the Heart

What better time to work on gifts for parents and friends than a bad weather day that keeps everyone inside? Some of these activities take several days or longer, so plan ahead a bit to allow plenty of time for children to see the projects through to the end.

Picture Perfect

Take each child's picture and get it developed and printed. Fold heavy colored paper to make a card for parents. Children can dip the palm of one hand in tempera paint and press it on the cover of the card. Inside, mount the photograph of each child. Add the date and the child's height and weight. Parents will keep these gifts forever.

Recipe for Fun

A collection of children's "recipes" makes a fun gift for parents, and creating it is fun for children, too. First sit together and place a food item from your cupboard or refrigerator in the center of the circle. For example, place a potato in the center and say, "Elizabeth, I want to make mashed potatoes. Can you tell me what to do with this potato to make them?" The children's responses will be priceless. Write them down, giving children credit for their contributions. Photocopy the results and staple them for a unique cookbook for parents.

So Big!

Before beginning this activity, have the children stand in front of a mirror to observe their own uniqueness. Then go to an area where the floor has a hard surface, like tile or wood. Use butcher paper cut 1 or 2 feet longer than each child is tall. Lay the paper on the floor and trace each child's body. Let the children color their self-portraits, adding hair, facial features, and clothes. Roll the pictures around wrapping paper tubes for easy transport home.

You Gotta Have Heart

Children enjoy giving greeting cards that they make themselves. Save canceled stamps, and ask parents to bring them from home and office, too. You'll need twenty-five stamps per child. Fold an $8\frac{1}{2}$-by-11-inch piece of construction paper in half to make each greeting card. From the front of the card, cut a heart shape about 4 inches across so that the front of the card has a heart-shaped hole in it. Children can use child-safe scissors to cut stamps from envelopes. They can then glue the stamps onto the heart-shaped pieces of paper. Stamps should overlap each other. It's okay if some stamps overlap the hearts; you can trim the edges later. Glue the trimmed hearts on the inside of the cards so the stamps show through the heart-shaped holes. Use markers to write the recipient's names on the front of the cards and to create scalloped edges for the hearts. Inside, outline the hearts with the markers and write the message "Your love is stamped all over my heart!"

Winter Lights

Help the children create a fresh, sweet-smelling candleholder to brighten a winter day. Use an apple corer or knife to make a hole in the stem end of a large apple with a flat bottom. (Don't cut it too wide, or the candle won't stand up.) Let the children place a candle in the hole. Snip pieces of evergreen 2 inches long. Remove needles from the bottom ½ inch of each evergreen stem. While children watch, use a toothpick to pierce the lower half of the apple at a slant. Continue all the way around the apple. Then let the children help you slide the ends of the evergreen pieces into the holes. Tie a bright ribbon at the base of the candle. The apple's juice keeps the evergreen fresh for a long time.

Gone Fishin'

A pencil cup with a fishing theme makes a great gift for someone who likes to fish. Use a clean, empty orange juice can or container of comparable size. The child glues blue or green wallpaper or construction paper around the outside. Next, using child-safe scissors, the child cuts a 1-inch-wide strip of paper in a contrasting color long enough to wrap around the outside of the can. Write a message to the gift recipient that says, "GRANDMA,

I'M HOOKED ON YOU!" Have the children glue the strip around the top edge of the can. Next, the child cuts a fish shape out of a piece of wallpaper or construction paper. Use a marker to draw scales on the fish. Make a dot where the fish's eye should be and where the child should cut for the wedge of its mouth. Let the child use a paper punch to make an eye (or leave the dot you drew). The child can cut the wedge for the mouth and glue the fish's body onto the front of the can so the head and tail stands away from the can. Help the child shape a pipe cleaner into a fishhook and glue it into place so that the hook catches the fish's mouth. Write the child's name and the date on the back of the cup.

See How I've Grown!

A growth record you've kept since the child first came to your home is a nice going-away gift for the parents of a child who is leaving your care. Every six months, take handprints of each child. For each child, use a piece of plain white shelf paper about 18 inches long. Pour tempera paint into a pie tin and spread it out with the back of a spoon. Dip the child's hand into the paint, palm side down. Press down on the child's hand at the left end of the paper. When dry, print the child's name, age, and the date below the handprint. Add a new handprint to the right of the previous one every six months. Send home on the last day the child is in your care.

Gift Tag Gifts

Children can make a set of four to six gift tags to give to their parents as a gift. Fold unlined 3-by-5-inch index cards in half and let the children use a paper punch to put a hole in the top folded corner. Children can use child-safe scissors to cut flower pictures from a seed catalog and glue them on the front of the gift tags. Leave the inside blank. Children can run a piece of ribbon through the hole, and tie.

IMPORTANT SAFETY TIP:
Be sure to use child-safe scissors and supervise their use.

Baked Beads

Children can help you make beads for a lovely gift necklace. With your help, the children can measure and mix $2\frac{1}{4}$ cups flour, 1 cup salt, and a couple packages of unsweetened Kool-Aid in a bowl. Add 1 cup of water and mix until the color is even and the clay is stiff. Pinch off pieces of clay and let the children roll them into beads. Then run a toothpick through the center of each bead. Stick one end of the toothpick into an egg carton or piece of Styrofoam. Let dry for a day or two, occasionally twirling the toothpick so that it doesn't stick to the inside of the bead. When the beads are dry, children can paint them with acrylic paint. When the paint is dry, move the beads away from the children's area and spray them with gloss-finish lacquer from a craft store. Let dry for a day. Children can then string the beads on fishing line. Be sure necklaces are long enough to fit over a person's head. Tie the ends of the fishing line in a knot.

Indoor Gardeners

This gift takes three to four weeks to bloom, so
plan ahead. Give each child a 16 ounce plastic
cup. Fill one-third of each cup with colored
aquarium gravel (rinse gravel first). Children set
paper white narcissis or hyacinth bulbs on the
gravel, then add more gravel, leaving the top
one-fifth of the bulb showing. They can then
pour enough water into the cup to cover the
bottom half of the bulb. Each day, have the children add 1 tablespoon of water. When the flowers bloom, tie ribbons around the cups and send
them home. Cover with plastic or tissue paper
to protect the blooms on the trip home.

Wrap It Up

Children can create their own wrapping paper to give as gifts or to use as
wrap for gifts they make. You'll need cardboard tubes, several large sheets
of white paper, and several colors of tempera paint. Cut the cardboard
tubes into 2½-inch lengths. Put thin layers of paint in separate bowls and
stir in three drops of Elmer's Glue to keep the paint from flaking when
dry. Have children dip one end of the cardboard tube into the paint and
stamp circles of it on the paper. Encourage the children's creativity. They
can make polka dots, overlap the circles, or use several different colors. If
they want to overlap circles or use more than one color on the same piece
of paper, let the paint dry between applying colors. Be sure the children
use a clean cardboard tube for each new color. (This is a great opportunity
for taking turns and sharing art supplies.)

Your Own Ideas

Use this space to write your own fun ideas.

About the Authors

Tina Koch

In addition to spending more than a decade as a family child care provider, Tina Koch has served as a child care center director, preschool teacher, and Head Start aide. Today she is a child care consultant and teacher-trainer on staff at The Day Care Connection, a nonprofit child care referral service and a sponsor of the U.S. Department of Agriculture's Child and Adult Care Food Program (CACFP) in Lenexa, Kansas. She also teaches child care classes at Johnson County Community College in Overland Park, Kansas. Tina is available for workshops, presentations, and keynote speaking at child care conferences and other training venues. She is coauthor of *Tips from Tina: Help Around the House* (St. Paul, MN: Redleaf Press, 1995).

Mary-Lane Kamberg

A professional writer for more than ten years, Mary-Lane Kamberg has published books and articles on a variety of topics including child care, parenting, health, education, and business. She received the John Phillip Immroth Memorial Award for 1996 from the Intellectual Freedom Round Table of the American Library Association. She is a fiction editor and member of the advisory board of Potpourri Publications and president of the board of directors of Whispering Prairie Press. She is coleader of the Kansas City Writers Group and leads writing workshops for writers' conferences and businesses. She has also taught writing classes at Johnson County Community College in Overland Park, Kansas. She is coauthor of *Tips from Tina: Help Around the House* (St. Paul, MN: Redleaf Press, 1995).

Also From Redleaf Press
Basic Resources for Your Family Child Care

The Basic Guide to Family Child Care Record Keeping - Easy-to-follow instructions on how to keep all your family child care business records.

The Business of Family Child Care with Tom Copeland - This introductory video covers the seven most important rules for record keeping, as well as taxes, insurance, contracts, and the Food Program.

Business Receipts for Child Care Services - Handy receipts designed specifically for family child care. Improve your record keeping and your professional image.

Calendar-Keeper - Streamline your record-keeping needs into a single calendar which also contains activities, recipes, menus, and more. Updated yearly.

Calendar-Keeper Cookbook - A great selection of 100 CACFP-approved recipes from 20 years of Redleaf's popular Calendar-Keeper make this cookbook a hit with providers and the kids in their care.

Family Child Care Contracts and Policies - Learn how to establish and enforce contracts and policies to improve your business.

Family Child Care Tax Workbook - Save time and money and calculate your taxes error free. Includes all new tax information for the year.

The (No Leftovers!) Child Care Cookbook - Contains over 80 kid-tested recipes and 20 complete menus with nutrition information—all CACFP approved. Ideal for larger home-based programs.

Room for Loving, Room for Learning - Put together the space that you need for yourself, your family, and the children in your care with this book full of ingenious ideas for better storage and activity areas.

Sharing in the Caring - A parent/provider agreement packet that helps you establish good business relationships and enhance your professional image. Also available are **Parent/Provider Policies**, actual forms you can use to create a thorough parent agreement, and **Medical Forms**, actual forms for documenting health and medical information on the children in your care—information that is required by most states.

Tips from Tina - Discover how to save yourself cleanup time and make routines more fun. Smooth schedules with these fresh solutions for those irritating, won't-go-away problems.

To order or for more information call
Redleaf Press
800-423-8309